Play-a-Sound™

COUNTING FUN

Illustrated by
Patrick Merrell

Written by
Judy Bruce and Jennifer Miller

Publications International, Ltd.

At Bedtime

Here's how to play:

The first column of buttons ask all the questions.
Each button asks lots of questions, so push each one over and over. This is Tiger's page.

The other buttons, like 3 or [shell], answer all the questions.
They tell you if you're right or wrong.
Let's begin! Press [Tiger] to hear questions about **At Bedtime**.

In Outer Space

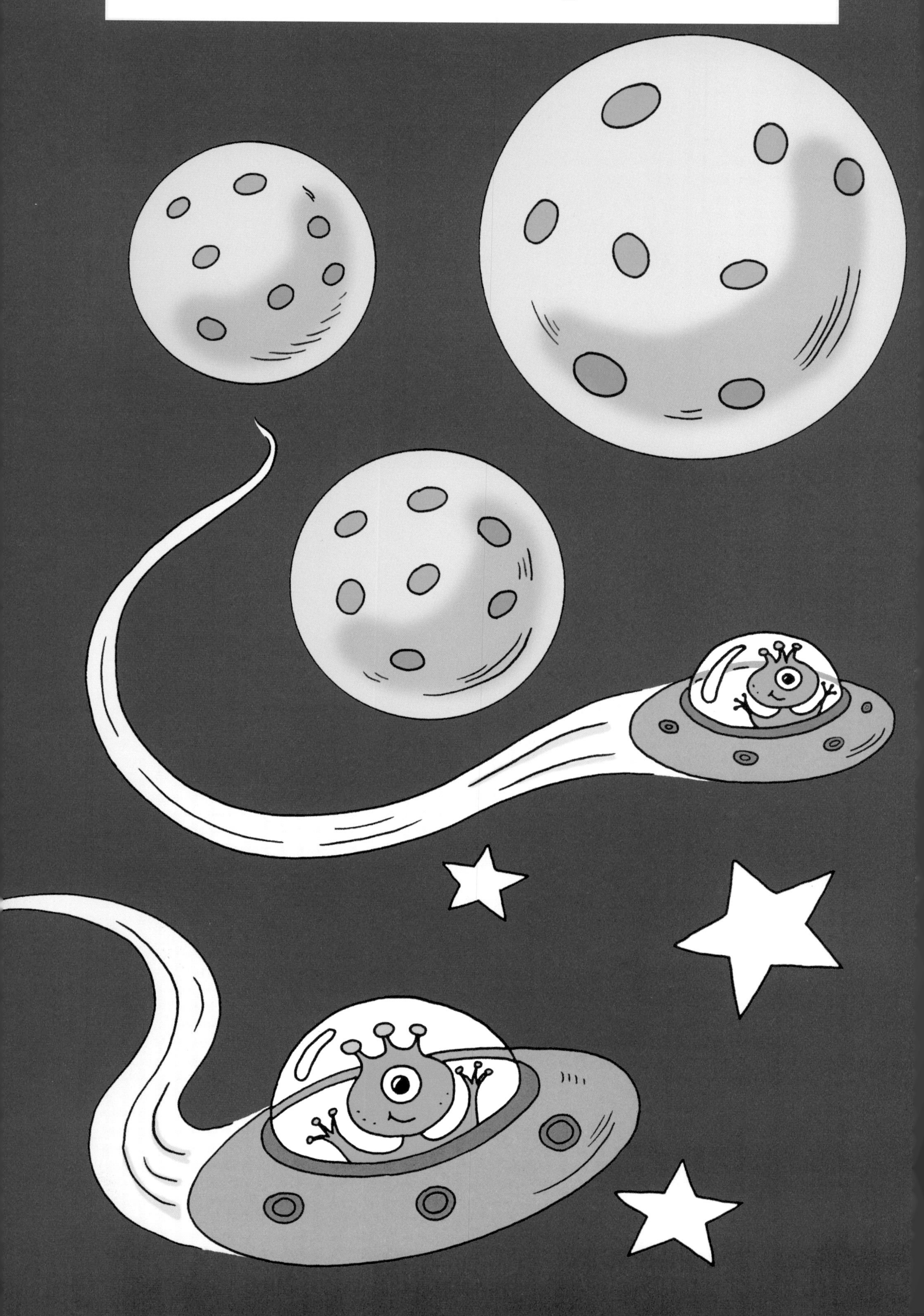

In the Bath

SOAP

Under the Ocean

Under the Bed

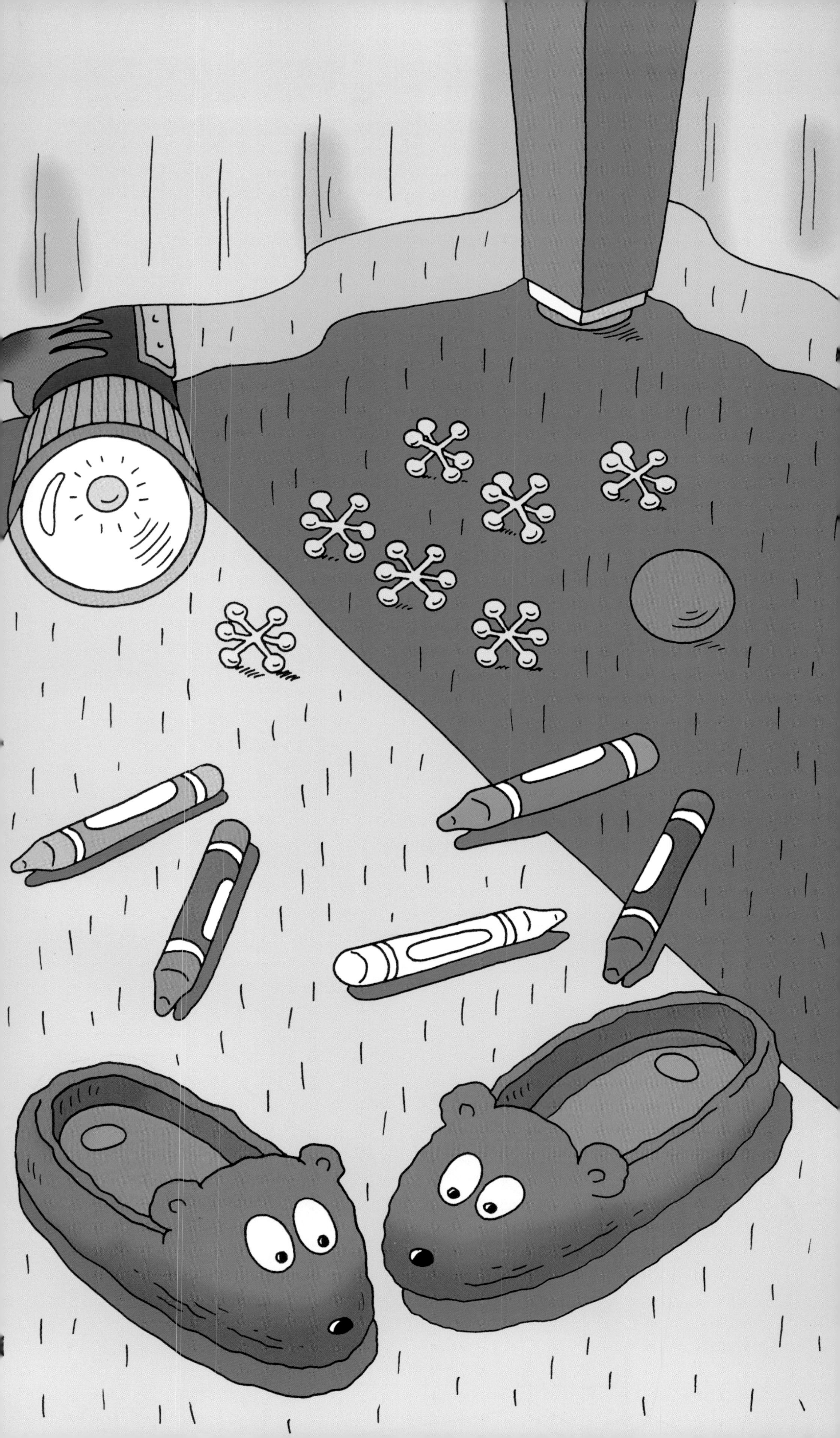

In the Cave

In the Sandbox

In the Castle

In the Birdbath

At Sea